TECHNICAL EDUCATION:

AN ADDRESS

DELIVERED BEFORE

The State Teachers' Association,

AT

SHIPPENSBURG, PENN'A.,

AUGUST 12, 1874.

BY

GEORGE WOODS, LL. D

PUBLISHED BY REQUEST.

PITTSBURGH:
BAKEWELL & MARTHENS, 71 GRANT STREET,
1874.

I ADDRESS the representatives of the nineteen thousand educators of our large, rich and influential State, to whom is entrusted the moulding of our twelve hundred thousand youth. Not our fertile soil or our many manufactures, in themselves considered, are of so much importance as the brain and brawn of the youth who are to cultivate this soil, and increase and perfect these manufactures, thus giving us the high rank we should attain among our sister States. However humble our work as teachers may be regarded by those who measure men by their annual income, or their display of dress and equipage, measured as every work should be, by the good done, it is second to none. I do not address legislators, sensitive as an aspen leaf to the popular breeze; or manufacturers, looking eagerly at the profits of the present year; but those who sow for others and the future; who toil, not to mine coal, or make pig-metal, but to build up true, intelligent men and women.

I address you on a practical subject, and I desire to do it as earnestly and with such statistics and facts as will impress you, and, through you, others in different parts of our State, with the great importance of the subject, and secure such action as shall advance the good of our youth and the interests of our State. And I propose to do it in a plain, unadorned manner, stating some of the many facts before me which favor education in the theory and practice of the arts and trades of all kinds, "that special education in our calling which should fit and enable each of us to discharge in the best manner the special narrow round of duty by which each citizen fills his own personal place in social life."

As teachers, our lives are not those of idleness or ease, but of severe, exhausting labor on material as varied in its nature as the different combinations of matter with the multiform elements of mind and heart, can make it.

To make an ingenious piece of machinery, requires labor and skill; to mould and fashion a soul, demands the exercise of the highest powers with which man is endowed. To create is the province of the Omnipotent; second only to this is it to develop that which allies man to the Creator. Education is "one of the greatest and noblest designs that can be thought on, and for which this nation perisheth." And yet the puddler, cutting tailor, glass-blower or sheet-worker, receives greater compensation than the soul-moulder, who fashions for eternity. More is paid for the covering than for the object covered; for the setting, than for the jewel.

Our duty as educators is not simply to instruct in one or a few studies, but to decide on the comparative value of different studies to different students, with different capacities, tastes, and purposes. The object to be moulded, and the use to be made of it, should be understood. What may be most useful to one at one time, may not be so at another time, or to another at the same time. The fit thing to be studied, in the fit quantity, at the fit time, is to be decided—what will be best suited to furnish, stimulate, and strengthen the mind for the future work. The question is not whether a certain study is useful or not, but whether it is the *most* useful for a certain student at a certain time, in his circumstances, and with his intended business or profession, and this, too, without reference to the taste, profit, or convenience of the teacher. To undervalue and disparage what we do not possess, is a fault no less common with the teacher than with others.

The study of the classics has been denounced as useless, and even injurious, a great waste of time. That they have been studied by those who should have devoted their time to other more practical studies, and by persons who had no taste or faculty which would enable them to be benefited by them, there can be no doubt. The same may be said of the higher mathematics, and many other studies. More time may have been wasted on the elementary English branches from commencing them at an improper time, studying portions comparatively valueless, and from defective teaching. The classics give us a knowledge of the sources of our modern culture, and, in no small measure, of our religion, polity, law, art and history. They are admirably suited to give us a knowledge of words, to improve the judgment, develop the mind, and to give finish and completeness to the man. All who would be accomplished scholars, or thorough professional men, and all who have the time and means, should study them.

The very men who ridicule and contemn the study of the classics as a waste of time, will teach other branches to such persons, and to such an extent or in such a manner as will prove an injury and loss to them. The youth who is to leave school at fourteen, is required to spend all or an unreasonable portion of his school life on unimportant parts of geography, grammar and arithmetic, to the total neglect of drawing. elementary chemistry, physics and other branches of knowledge, an acquaintance with which is essential to his success in life. The acknowledged waste of time on the classics by those who have no time or capacity for them, or who pursue them to the neglect of more important studies, is, however, sustained by comparatively few; the loss from entire neglect, or injudicious teaching of many of the primary branches, is sustained by the many. Less than four per cent. of our youth extend their studies beyond the common elementary branches. An error, therefore, in our educational methods, for these branches affect twenty-four times as many persons as in the case of the classics. So, while gazing at distant objects, we have stumbled into holes immediately before us. Such is human consistency!

The relative worth of different kinds of knowledge to the student has not been sufficiently regarded. The studies he has pursued may be valuable, and to the extent to which he has pursued them, whilst they may be less so than other studies that might have been substituted in whole or in part. An immense amount of information bearing on the industrial activities, which should be understood by all, has been passed over, while the less useful has been studied. There has been a tendency to regard the useful as ignoble.

The answer, then, to the question, What should our youth study? has not been intelligently given. The philosopher said they should study that which they will most need when they become men. William Penn, in writing to his wife in relation to the education of his children, said, "Give them learning, but let it be useful learning." The people are generally convinced, now, that the classics have occupied an unreasonably large part of the time of many, and that studies having a closer connection with the intended pursuits of our youth will be more useful. The opposing current has fully set in. Care should be taken that we do not go to the opposite extreme, seeking only the immediately practical. Universities do not exist merely for the purpose of training men for their special crafts or trades. To ridicule any ulterior end is irrational. "The man is more than the trade." Practical, skilful men in the trades and arts we need. To have them we must educate them. They will not grow of themselves. God will not work a wonder to help us when he has given us wherewith to help ourselves. Especially are such men demanded in *our* State, where there are so many persons engaged in agricultural, mechanical, engineering and mining pursuits. To advocate such an education is to advocate the highest interests of our Commonwealth and its toilers.

The opinions of men as to the comparative value of studies, have varied greatly at different periods. Archimedes regarded it as degrading to science to be useful, to contribute to the wants and happiness of man. According to Seneca, to impute to man any share in the invention or improvement of a plow, a ship, or a mill, was an insult. It is in accordance with this spirit that practical studies, those which relate to the daily employments of life, are now stigmatized as "bread and butter sciences." In the Middle Ages alchemy, astrology and dialectics were the cardinal studies. In the latter part of this period, Gerard Groot, a mighty preacher in the mother tongue, said, "Spend no time on geometry, arithmetic, rhetoric, dialectics, grammar, poetry, horoscopes, or astrology. Such pursuits are renounced by

Seneca, much more by Christians of a spiritual mind. They avail not for the spiritual life." About the same time Hegius said, "If any one wishes to understand grammar, rhetoric, mathematics, history or the Holy Scriptures, let him study Greek. We owe everything to the Greeks." At a later period, Latin was recommended for all. Being the repository of the learning of the world, it is not strange that a knowledge of it should have been required of all students. In 1854, President Francis Wayland, one of the best educators and noblest men our country has ever had, having eight years before expressed his dissatisfaction with the then existing course of study, in an address at Union College, said: "It would seem that our whole system of instruction needs an honest, thorough and candid revision. It has been for centuries the child of precedent. If those before us made it what it is, by applying to it the resources of earnest and fearless thought, I can see no reason why we, by precisely the same course, might not improve it. God intended us for progress, and we counteract his designs when we deify antiquity and bow down and worship an opinion, not because it is either wise or true, but simply because it is ancient."

Soon after this, Prof. Chase, of Brown University, gave eight lectures to three hundred and fifty-three jewelers and other workers in metal, on "The Chemistry of the Precious Metals." These lectures gave great satisfaction and profit, and remarks were made by the workmen showing how much they felt they had lost by not having received such instruction before.

In 1858, that invaluable article, "What knowledge is of the most worth?" gave a fresh impulse to the new departure. To answer this question of Herbert Spencer wisely, and to give to all the students in our schools, colleges and universities, the knowledge of most worth to them, should be the object of all educators. So multiplied have the sciences become, and so increased the range of studies, that we cannot compel the student to follow a routine suited to past centuries. The two different opinions as to the object of education still prevail; Froude says it is to prepare the student to obtain his food and clothing; Matthew Arnold says: "To know is sublime; to do, base." To recognize the change that has taken place, and adapt ourselves to it, is the part of wisdom. We cannot sympathize with the distinguished Greek scholar, who, on his death-bed, lamented that he had not spent the last twenty years of his life on the dative case.

The old and rich institutions of England are slow to adapt themselves to the changes in learning. In Cambridge, it is said, a man may yet get the highest honors in mathematics and natural philosophy, and have never seen a crystal, a lens, an air-pump, or a thermometer; and at Oxford he may get his first honor in natural science without knowing the binomial theorem or the solution of a triangle. Yet in technical education we are far behind England and the continent, where are numerous richly endowed institutions fitted to give instruction in practical education. They have consequently acquired great superiority over us in many of the arts and manufactures. We have been too well satisfied with ourselves and our school system, and have not educated our youth in the arts so as to develop without "trial and error," and without the most lavish waste, our abundant natural resources. Our wealth has reached the sum of $30,000,000,000. But we forget that we are in most cases exhausting our virgin soil without seeking to restore it; that we are consuming our vast stores of mineral wealth and recklessly destroying our forests. In one year, 1870, this transfer of wealth from the surface and from beneath the surface, after deducting the cost of labor and material, was $1,183,-410,861, or one twenty-fifth of all our computed wealth. We took our riches from the earth, and, aided by foreign capital to the amount of $1,400,-000,000—our supposed entire foreign indebtedness—we erected our edifices, built our ships and railroads, and fancied ourselves more wealthy by this entire amount. We forgot that the change of a dollar from the purse to the hand, where it could be seen and counted, is not an increase of one dollar in our wealth. It was a dollar, and is a dollar still. We forgot that it is labor which creates wealth or enhances values, and, so far as labor was employed in developing our resources, to that amount, and to that amount only, it has added to our wealth. Of this vast natural wealth we must not be too prodigal. We have, it is true, one of the richest countries on the earth; a fertile soil, extensive forests, and an abundance of oil, coal, iron, salt, gold, silver, lead, copper, nickel, slate and marble. Much of our soil has already been exhausted through bad agriculture. We are less careful in this respect than the Chinese, who see that every element taken from the soil is returned to it, so that there shall be no waste. Our woodlands have been so recklessly stripped, noble forests often girdled and left to stand for years to decay, monuments of our wastefulness, that the cry, Forbear! is coming up from all parts of our land.

Our iron and coal, too, have been used without regard to economy. What we want is to use all our abundant material so economically as to have no waste, and to apply to it so much of skilled labor as will add the most possible to its value, The labor, too, should be applied in this and not in foreign countries. To send our cotton to England and bring it back, paying for it many times what we received, or to send over our wheat to be converted into labor, is doing what England did from Alfred to Edward the Confessor—selling our skins for a sixpence, and buying the tails for a shilling. We have no faith in the opinion, early expressed in our country, that we should confine ourselves to agriculture and avoid manufactures. This would make us the slaves of foreign countries, simply tributary to their wealth. An agricultural people can never become wealthy or powerful. What we do want is intelligent, skilled labor to enhance the value of the natural wealth of the country, and send it to the market increased in value one hundred or a thousand fold. How greatly labor increases the value of the material, can be easily illustrated. Aniline colors, surpassing in beauty the Tyrian purple, are made from coal tar, until lately a worthless refuse; and the aniline blue sells for $28 a pound. A pound of cotton, costing 12 cents, made into muslin of good design, sells for 80 cents, and into chintz, $4; a pound of the finest cotton, costing 40 cents, made into cotton lace, will bring $1,000. Iron ore, costing 75 cents, made into bar iron, will sell for $5; horse shoes, $10.50; table knives, $180; the finest needles, $6,800; shirt buttons, $29,480; watch springs, $200,000; hair springs, $400,000; pallet arbors, $2,577,595. Here labor has, with the aid of machinery, produced the difference between 75 cents and $2,577,595. Any article obtained without labor has no exchangeable value. Rude labor, that which requires no practice or education, brings the lowest price; dexterous labor, which enables a person through practice to perform works or parts of works quickly and nicely, brings a higher price; and skilled labor, combining a knowledge of the principles underlying the operation, as well as dexterity in their execution, brings the highest price. Skilled labor creates values, rude labor often destroys them. The last stroke of the skilled sculptor gives value to the statue; one blow of the rude laborer might destroy the work of years. It is by labor that our machine-shops and iron-furnaces have been productive of more wealth to our State than would be the richest gold mines of the world. And if one-half of the 616,000 persons in our State engaged in agriculture, manufactures, and mechanical and mining industries, should become *skilled* laborers, there would be an annual addition to our wealth of $184,800,000. If there should be the same change in one-half of the 9,000,000 engaged in the same pursuits in our whole country, it would, at a very low estimate, add $2,700,000,000 annually to the wealth of the nation. We must not overlook the fact that the sum required for necessary food and clothing, is the same for all classes of laborers. In England it has been computed that $125 represents the cost of a highly skilled over a skilless workman; and that this cost of a skilled workman is less than one year's purchase of his increased value to the nation.

A single fact will illustrate the value of skilled labor in producing the best machinery. A Pittsburgh cotton manufacturing company wanted a new Corliss steam engine to take the place of one they then had. The offer of one for $8,500 was refused. A second offer, for the fuel saved in five years by the use of the new engine, disclosed the fact that the saving would be $200 per month, or $12,000 in five years. The engine was taken at the first offer. The saving from machinery running evenly, avoiding the breaking of threads, was probably equal to the saving of fuel.

Time will not permit us to do more than to allude to the vast losses arising from ignorant and incompetent workmen, engineers, architects, overseers, or owners of property. The abandoning on the ocean of the French steamship L'Amerique through the ignorance of the engineer; the building by our own government, at a cost of $11,000,000, of twenty light-draft monitors, not large enough to carry the turrets for which they were intended; the placing of an engine at the cost of nearly $800,000, on one of our government ships, which was abandoned after a single voyage to San Domingo, in which the lives of many illustrious men were endangered; the Pemberton mills disaster, in which of the seven hundred and fifty employees eighty-eight were killed, and many disabled for life; the recent Mill River disaster, costing one hundred and fifty lives and $2,000,000; the falling of a floor in a Syracuse church, killing instantly fourteen, and injuring one hundred more; these losses are familiar to all. Large sums and many lives are lost by incompetent railroad engineers and architects. Soils are exhausted, and small crops are gathered, through ignorance of the chemical and mechanical principles involved in agriculture. We are now taking annually nearly $600,000,000 in value from the elements of our soil, and it has been said that we have taken more in value than the entire wealth of the country. Agriculture is fast becoming chemistry, and husbandry, machinery.

When men understand the theory as well as practice of their business, there will be less time and money wasted in futile attempts at inventions directly at variance with well-established laws. Inventions, of which we have many, as the thirteen thousand patents granted last year show, are generally the result of scientific knowledge. We have already placed England under obligations to our inventions to the amount of $1,000,000,000. But the seven thousand rejected applications for patents last year prove that there has been much misapplied time and ingenuity in this direction. We are almost daily reminded of the folly of the man who, by years of labor, sought to propel a boat by taking water into the bow and ejecting it from the stern. The $20,000 lost in the vain attempt to collect the alcohol from bread in baking, and the efforts to construct electro-magnetic engines in the hope of superseding steam, are examples of the same kind. I have often been compelled to advise young men to abandon useless projects to which they had devoted years of patient toil and all their means. A knowledge of scientific principles would have saved them this loss. Science often comes to the rescue of ignorance, though sometimes at a late hour. The pretended discovery of diamonds in California was exposed by Clarence King, but not until innocent men had been defrauded of hundreds of thousands of dollars. The Nevada fraud was revealed to the public by a young scientist, saving $1,000,000. A graduate of a scientific school, for a fee of $250, showed the iron mines of New York, in which hundreds of thousand of dollars were invested, to be valueless in consequence of containing titanium, thus saving $400,000.

It must be remembered that what was economy fifty years ago, is gross wastefulness now, and what is economy now, will be regarded as reckless prodigality fifty years hence. From the waste of former years fortunes are now made. Less than forty years ago, Dr. Buckland said: "We have during many years witnessed the disgraceful and almost incredible fact that more than 36,000,000 bushels, per annum, more than one-third part of the best coals produced by the mines near Newcastle, have been condemned to wanton waste, on a fiery heap perpetually blazing near the mouth of almost every pit in that coal district." All the small coal was disposed of in this manner. Dr. Buckland said the inevitable consequence of this frightful waste would be to exhaust this coal field one-third sooner than it would be exhausted if wisely economized, and to endanger the interests of the inhabitants who depend for existence on machinery kept in action by coal. England to-day realizes the justice of this warning in her perilled manufactures. Carrying coals to Newcastle formerly expressed an absurdity; now, a fact. In this country it is now wisely proposed to consume all the coal dust.

J. Scott Russell, the builder of the Great Eastern, from his own experience, says: "The community at large are deprived of enormous treasures in mechanical inventions and enormous progress in scientific arts, by the fact of the general want of education in those who practice them. It may not be known, but it is yet true, that the mechanical power employed in all our manufactures is infinitely more costly than it need be. It is equally true that some skilled men know thoroughly how to produce immense economy in the production and use of mechanical power, but that we dare not put the means into the hands of uneducated masters under whose control they would be applied. I am not speaking of a loss of 5, 10, 20 or 30 per cent.; I say that we know that we are only utilizing one-tenth to one-twentieth of the power we employ and waste, and that an economy of 100, 200, 300 and 400 per cent. is quite within our power, so soon as a better-informed, higher-skilled, more perfectly trained class of men and masters shall arise, who are fitted to be trusted with the use of instruments and tools, at present utterly beyond their comprehension, control, or application to use."

And again he says: "I find everywhere throughout the work of the railroads of the continent marks of that method, order, symmetry and absence of waste which arise from plans well thought out, the judicious application of principles, conscientious parsimony and a high feeling of professional responsibility."

Such practical and theoretical education as I am advocating, will save many of the losses arising from ignorance, or a want of habits of thought. Property and life will be preserved, the nation will be enriched, and the fierceness of the struggle between labor and capital will be diminished. What benefits the State benefits her citizens. Better educated and more skilled workmen command higher compensation, and higher compensation will enable men to procure more comforts and luxuries, and to take higher positions among their fellows. A person educated in the common branches alone will usually earn twice the sum that an uneducated one will, and then his prospects are good for advancement to the position of overseer or manager, with, it may be, a salary of thousands, while the ignorant man has no such chance. A few years since, a director of one of the extensive cotton manufacturing corporations at Lowell, Mass., stated that only forty-five out of twelve hundred operatives in their mills were unable to write their names, and that the wages of these were twenty-seven per cent. less than the wages of those who could write. In the same mills were one hundred and fifty girls who had been teachers. Their wages were seventeen and three-fourths per cent. above the general average, and forty per cent. above those who made their mark.

But it cannot fail to have been observed that a mere theoretical knowledge will not secure success in a profession or manufacture. To know that an experiment or operation can be performed, and to perform it, are quite different. We havė seen many and grand failures, and large sums lost from an error here. The theory of navigation would not ensure a safe captain on the ocean. Many currents and their rates, many winds and their effects, and many peculiarities of his own ship, must be known.

Power to think, combined with a thorough practical knowledge of mechanics and the principles of science, will enable one to manage machinery skilfully, economizing labor, and increasing its effectiveness. Machinery everywhere is performing the most delicate and the most powerful operations, from the spinning of the slenderest thread to the making of the massive iron plate. It must be directed by intelligence and thought, and the greater the improvement in machinery, the greater the intelligence and skill required to manage it. To-day, with the aid of machinery, one girl spins as much as did three thousand of the sun-stained Hindoos centuries ago. It has been estimated that, at the present time, the laborers of Europe and the United States, with the aid of machinery, are doing four times the work that the whole population of the globe could do by direct labor.

Machinery in the varied manufactures enables all, of whatever taste or strength, to find remunerative employment, which is essential to the prosperity of a nation. Agriculture calls for only a small part of the laborers, and those of well-developed muscles. Already our manufactures are many and varied, amounting annually to $4,000,000,000, double our agricultural products. In our State, the value of our manufactures for 1870 was $711,894,344, and our agricultural products were only $183,946,027. In many articles we already equal or surpass other nations. Of seventy-six classes of articles manufactured in Birmingham, England, the chairman of the Association of Commerce states that twenty-four are replaced in the common markets of the world by the United States. Our cut nails, sewing machines, pumps and edge tools are unsurpassed by those of any other nation. We have orders for table glass from Europe; our cotton fabrics are sent over the world; Bigelow's looms for weaving carpets are unrivalled. We have $10,000,000 invested in the ceramic art in a single city, and have in our country every needed variety of clay for the most complete success in this large branch of industry. We are now filling a large order for locomotives for Russia. Our silk manufactures in 1872 reached the sum of $25,000,000, affording remunerative employment to eleven thousand seven hundred and thirteen men and women, while our importations of this article of luxury have fallen to $24,000,000, a reduction of $10,000,000 in three years. To affect contempt for an American silk now, is to betray ignorance of its value. We are taking annually from England 150,000 tons of tin at the exorbitant price of $115,200,000, foolishly allowing her a monopoly in this article, while possessing mines in our own country, and yet, to her astonishment, we send back tin-ware. By increasing our manufactures, we should stop so large importations of woolen goods as $52,408,921 in 1872, and larger importations of other textiles, books, wares and numerous luxuries for which we pay annually many millions. These industries should be multiplied, and technical education will tend to this result, by giving us the skilled workmen needed for this work. The almost entire disappearance of the apprenticeship system, and the oppressive rules of trades-unions, make this education an imperative necessity. Our manufacturers would gladly listen to the entreaties of fathers and mothers to take their sons as apprentices, but they cannot.

The State must remedy this evil, or suffer our youth to become common laborers under foreign overseers. England until 1868 neglected this education, and so fell behind the Continent, losing her position in the manufacture of many articles. The shawl trade of Leeds was absorbed by continental manufacturers by reason of their technical knowledge; the silk trade was injured by a superior skill in dye and finish on the Continent; the designers, dyers and engravers in foreign countries, by possessing a thorough theoretical and practical knowledge of their several trades, produced greater purity and beauty of design, cleaner and brighter colors in the cloths and other fabrics they manufactured, finer patterns and greater lightness; Coventry ribbons were taken from her; foreign workmen were employed as painters and designers, and great deficiencies existed in those branches of knowledge which bear most intimately on the great departments of industry. Alarmed at these discoveries—that she was losing her supremacy in manufactures, that French companies were building locomotives for an English railway, and that iron girders for a building in Glasgow were being constructed in Belgium, she at once established technical schools of a high order in the large cities, with others of a lower grade in the smaller towns. For a single department of the art school in South Kensington, £1,000,000 were expended, and £80,000 annually were given for its support by the state. In Queen's Institute, Belfast, Ireland, from three hundred to four hundred female students are trained in all branches of skilled labor, for which taste and physical fitness make them suitable.

In Europe these schools are many, and are supported wholly or in part by the state, on a scale, too, worthy the object. In 1869 there were three hundred and fifty technical schools in Paris. Eleven thousand men receive a technical education annually in Prussia. From ten thousand to twelve thousand workmen attend the lectures of the University in Berlin. Creuzot is a wonder of activity, skill and success, from her systematic technical education. From the same cause, Switzerland, cut off from the sea and from mines, with her mountain climate, at every disadvantage, competes with the world in many of her manufactures. In our own country, Cooper Institute, Stevens Institute, the Worcester Free Institute, and the Institute of Technology in Boston, and many colleges and universities, are doing valuable service in this department.

That there should be some change in our course of education, conforming to the increased extent of the sciences and their numerous applications, must be evident. What shall the change be? What reforms shall be introduced in our present studies, and what new studies shall be adopted? Time will permit me to make only a few suggestions in reply to these important questions.

The primary school should give a knowledge of objects, their forms and colors and uses. In doing this, drawing will be found highly useful, and it will prove an agreeable change from studies less interesting. It is, too, the foundation of technical education, and is important to all of every trade and profession.

By training the eye to keenness, and the hand to accuracy and rapidity, it will prove a valuable aid to penmanship, orthography and reading, in all of which close observation is necessary. In its higher forms, geometric, model, mechanical and architectural, it should be continued through the higher schools and colleges. It is not mere picture-drawing of which I speak, but something higher and more useful. As a result of this study, we shall have better artists, engineers, mechanics, architects, and designers. Many articles, such as glass, pottery, cabinet furniture, prints, and other manufactures, may be rendered worthless, or have their values increased manyfold, according to their designs. Good designs increase the value of prints from twenty to thirty per cent. So important is this art of designing considered now, that a firm in New York pays a designer in shoes $5,000 a year. By the beauty of his designs a manufacturer of silverware in Taunton, Mass., drove every other manufacturer out of the market. A single manufacturing company in Massachusetts stated that their designs cost them $40,000 annually, every dollar of which went to England, France and Germany. This sum should be saved to our own country.

Workmen do not sufficiently understand the importance of drawing. It is said that if this art were understood by every journeyman in a machine shop, the productive efficiency would be increased thirty-three per cent. By enabling workmen to work from a design instead of expensive models, this art would save a vast amount of time and money. A manager of an important branch of industry at Worcester, Massachusetts, says that, when a lad, he was one of a class of thirteen, who spent all their leisure time in studying drawing. At the present time, every one then in the class has attained an important position either as manufacturer or manager, and each has owed his power to seize the opportunity of advancement, to his knowledge of drawing.

Massachusetts, ever alive to her educational and manufacturing interests, finding that she was far behind Europe in the education of her laborers, and that, as a consequence, her industries were suffering, adopted drawing as one of the studies to be taught in all the public schools of the State, making it obligatory on every city containing over ten thousand inhabitants to furnish free instruction in this art to all over fifteen years of age. An art director was procured from Europe at a salary of $5,000, and generous provisions were, in all respects, made. The result is most gratifying. In 1870, her product in printed cottons was over $17,000,000, and her other manufactures in which design is of the first importance, were probably more. Massachusetts never made a better investment for her sons and daughters, and her manufacturing interests.

It is believed that this study can be introduced

into our schools without interfering at all with the present lines of study. Familiar lectures, with illustrations, on geometry, elementary physics, elementary chemistry and natural history, should be given to all who are to leave school early. The amount of scientific information thus received, though it may be small, will lead the pupils to notice facts and to study principles in science throughout life. As the pupils advance, as far as practicable, models or drawings of machinery, or the machinery itself, and all processes of manufacture, should be examined, and reports made with drawings explaining them, showing their excellencies or defects, and suggesting remedies. Special schools, or departments in existing schools, should be established where these branches may be thoroughly taught. As soon as it can be done, shops should be erected, where certain trades or parts of trades can be learned, where the hand and eye can be trained, and the student prepared for work or the management of works. Those who take a higher course in our schools and universities, should receive thorough instruction in all the sciences which relate to engineering, agriculture, the arts, trades and manufactures. It is my opinion, confirmed by many educators of experience and good judgment, that much of the time—years, it may be—now devoted to a few primary studies, reviewed so often that the process becomes mechanical and positively injurious, may be saved by commencing each study at the proper age, and omitting unnecessary portions of the text-books. Occasionally, for a term, the study of arithmetic, geography or grammar, may be wholly omitted for some new and more interesting study relating to science or the arts. The experiments and illustrations will awaken mind, kindle enthusiasm, and many will be induced to prolong their attendance at school, who otherwise would not. By this course far more will be accomplished in a given time than now. It has been found that students who have spent but two hours per day in study, and the remaining hours in labor in which they felt an interest, have often made as much proficiency in their studies as those who have devoted their whole time to study.

Those whose course of study is to be limited to fourteen or sixteen years of age—and these compose by far the largest part of our students—should have a short, practical course, in accordance with such limited time. All, of whatever capacity or purpose, should *not* be compelled to pursue the same routine in the same time. This is the very objection brought so justly against the old collegiate system. Yet while that system in many colleges has been so much changed as to embrace numerous distinct courses suited to the different students, and in addition, in one case at least, to offer more than forty optional studies, there has not been a corresponding change in most of our grammar and ward schools.

Our best authorities agree that our public school

system, so well adapted to a former state of society, fails to meet the wants of our people in the present state of civilization. And while there is a demand to extend our course of education upwards so as to embrace all the sciences, let us seek to extend it downwards to the practical, the Kindergarten, in all our primary and grammar schools. What is demanded of the college, let the public school practice. A loss of two or three years to a student in our public schools, who has but a few years of study, is far more to him than the same number of years to the collegiate student, whose course may extend to his twenty-second or twenty-fifth year. Let not the student, fitted by capacity and taste to excel in some one branch of knowledge or art, be compelled to spend all his school years on studies, valuable, it is true, yet having no special bearing on his future pursuit, on which all his interests centre. A failure to arouse the mind of the student, and to communicate to him that knowledge which he may most need in life, may be fatal to his whole future.

If a reform is needed, our educators should endeavor to effect it at once, so that there may be as little loss as possible. Let us not be "the last by whom the new is tried." A great work lies before us. Public opinion is to be formed, legislators are to be instructed, and large expenditures to be made by the State or individuals. In a cause which will yield such large returns the State can afford to expend liberally.

Some special schools have already been established on a comparatively limited scale, and many of our colleges, where the change commenced in this country, have their scientific departments. The effects of these practical and theoretical technical schools, wherever established, have been most marked—stimulating the intellect to activity, and diminishing the poverty, vice and crime of the community. And when we consider that eighty-two per cent. of the criminals of our country never learned any trade, never were masters of any skilled labor, and only six per cent. are skilled artisans and mechanics, the ethical value of this education becomes exceedingly important. The professions are crowded, and manufacturing and mechanical and agricultural pursuits are less honored than they should be. Our fathers and mothers should feel that a practical technical education is what most of their sons and daughters need. Our youth should be taught that there is true dignity in skilled manual labor, and that it will bring liberal pecuniary returns.

To woman, rapidly rising to her true position, to whom the avenues of trade, the professions, and all kinds of employment are opening, this subject appeals with peculiar force. She should have a deep interest in any measure which will render her less dependent on husband, brother or father, and which will enable her to obtain a generous support when other resources fail. She should seek to be in a condition to feel independent, and to be able with ease to earn a livelihood. A knowledge of some art will tend to give her a higher position and to secure for her higher respect. From her knowledge of colors and their relations, and her skill in drawing, woman is fitted to succeed in whatever requires taste. The success of the lady pupils at South Kensington is greater than that of the male students, and that in the face of greater difficulties. The many branches of art—workmanship requiring delicate fingers and native readiness of taste, can be better performed by woman than by man. In 1859, twenty thousand women were employed in watch-making in Switzerland. Our silk manufacturers employ seven thousand eight hundred and two women, in light, clean, remunerative work. A lady in Pittsburgh receives $250 per month for designs in embroidery, made wholly by herself. Woman can excel in draughting, architectural drawing, photography, engraving, modeling, designing and painting. Education in the arts, by opening to her new departments of labor, will enable her better to compete with man, secure for her better compensation for her services, and will increase her usefulness and influence.

For the proper education of all our youth, with the least loss—the education that will best fit them for the duties of life, I plead. I do not, while speaking in behalf of practical learning, forget the moral and the religious training, without which man will be a failure here and hereafter. The heart is more than the hand or eye—the future more than the present. Ability, power, may be used for evil instead of good; to curse instead of to bless. To others I must entrust this subject. I plead for useful learning in the school-room or the shop, or both, as a means of interesting our youth, giving them a taste for manual pursuits, so restraining them from idleness and crime; of enabling them to provide better for their own comfort and happiness, so increasing their self-respect and adding to the wealth and moral power of the State.

The effects of technical education in Europe lead us to believe that this system, commenced in the primary school, and continued through the different grades, would bring many of the five million youth in our country of school age, who attend no school, under instruction, and make them industrious, moral, happy and skilled laborers, instead of paupers and criminals.

When plans for education in all its departments, for all, shall be wisely devised and faithfully executed, we shall have better and more productive workmen, better citizens, thinking men and women, multiplied power of machinery economically used, the yield of our soil doubled, a more virtuous people, and our republic more prosperous and more safe.

www.ingramcontent.com/pod-product-compliance
Lightning Source LLC
LaVergne TN
LVHW011133110826
845150LV00008B/2326

* 9 7 8 1 4 1 8 1 9 4 5 7 4 *